Story Octopus

Writing Helper Extraordinaire

Written and Illustrated by Carole "Lisa Lynn" Gilbert
Co-Illustrated by Brielle Casillas

Copyright 2019. All rights reserved.

ISBN 978-0-6929845-8-1 (sc)
ISBN 978-0-6921103-1-7 EPUB

For Vanessa and the staff at her school
For the opportunity to be creative
For their Career Day,
And to all the kids there
And everywhere.

I like to write stories.
I like to have fun.
I want to show you how.
Together we'll work on one.
Whether at home or school, writing is fun.
I'll give you the tools for a job well done.

My stories are made up
Full of imagination.
Please join me and let's
Write our own creation.

These are my legs.
They take me
Where I go.
They're with me from
The start to end.
And that's where
Our story begins.

Then using
My six arms
We'll tell
A lot.

So in the beginning,
Is your story on
land, air, or sea?

Who's the main
character?
How many
will there be?

When is your story happening? What message do you want to send?

Why are you telling this tale? How will it end?

So many questions
To decide and jot down.
Use me for an example,
Giving me a smile or a frown.

What would it be, A
story from you?
Happy or sad,
Fiction or true?

Would you
Give me a hat?
Some kind of
Ball or a cat?

Groceries

Would you take me to a store?

Would you be My friend Forevermore?

Decide all the details
Your story has begun.
From beginning to end
You'll have imaginary fun!
Thank you for writing
With me today.
Keep up the creative work
You're well on your way!

Glossary of Writing Terms:

Genre- the kind or type of story (examples-fiction, nonfiction, children's, novel).

Beginning- the start of a story.

Middle- the central part of a story.

End- goal; result or achievement of a story; resolution.

Character (Characters) - the "who" in a story.

Plot- the events that make up the main part of a story.

"What" is to happen, explain or describe, and "How" do you know.

Setting- "where" and "when" does the story take place.

Conflict- struggle between characters; point or purpose to a story; the "why" of a story.

Climax- the most intense point of action in a story.

Editing- to correct and prepare.

Illustrate- drawings and pictures that help you explain your story.

Your Story…

Who _____

_____

_____

_____

_____

_____

_____

What _____

_____

_____

_____

_____

_____

_____

_____

Where_____

_____

_____

_____

_____

_____

When_____

_____

Why

How_____

_____

_____

_____

_____

_____

_____

_____

Happy Writing!

Story Octopus: Writing Helper Extraordinaire

Carole "Lisa Lynn" Gilbert is a wife, mom, Gma, and award winning Christian author. Story Octopus was created for a Career Day at a local Elementary School. Carole's love for imagination soars back to her childhood whims and her knowledge of writing and publishing made Story possible and available to all.

Co-Illustrator Brielle Casillas is the six year old granddaughter of Carole "Lisa Lynn" Gilbert. In her spare time, after school, Brielle likes to play, do gymnastics, and draw.

Story Octopus helps children learn to write, a tool used in every aspect of our lives, through creativity and imagination. Story includes pages at the end of his book for your child to start their own creative work as he guides and motivates.

www.ingramcontent.com/pod-product-compliance
Lightning Source LLC
Chambersburg PA
CBHW041326290426
44110CB00004B/152